All Henry's children would go on to rule England, but Mary and Elizabeth were particularly unusual as they were the first female rulers of England. There had been queens of England before, but it was always their husbands who really ruled the country.

But the journey to becoming queen was not a simple one for either of these half-sisters.

Catherine Parr

Catherine Howard

First wife, first child

One of the main reasons why things were complicated for Henry's children was that Henry married six times. Mary, Elizabeth and Edward each had a different mother.

Mary's mother was Katherine of Aragon, a Spanish princess. She married Henry in 1509, the same year that he became king of England, and Mary was born in 1516.

Henry's first wife, Katherine of Aragon

Mary, *aged around nine,*
before her troubles began

Mary was a much-loved daughter and she had
a happy childhood. Her mother made sure that she had
the best education possible – she was playing musical
instruments for people visiting her father from the age of
four and could read and write Latin by the age of nine.

The break with Rome

Things started to go wrong for Mary when Henry became desperate to have a son. He wanted to create a Tudor dynasty in which members of his family would rule England for years to come. He felt that this was much more likely if he passed his crown on to a man. At the time, women were seen as weaker and less capable than men.

After years of failing to have the son he wanted, Henry began to think about divorce. He'd fallen in love with one of Katherine's maids, Anne Boleyn, and he was convinced that she'd give him a son. To get divorced from Katherine so that he could marry Anne, Henry needed special permission from the **Pope**, but the Pope refused.

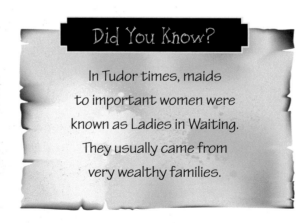

Did You Know?

In Tudor times, maids to important women were known as Ladies in Waiting. They usually came from very wealthy families.

the first meeting
of Henry the Eighth
and Anne Boleyn

7

Henry didn't give up and decided that the only way to get his divorce was to set up his own church, the Church of England, with himself as its leader. This removed the Pope's control of the church in England and meant Henry could make sure that permission for his divorce was given.

Clement the Seventh, the Pope who refused to give Henry his divorce

Anne Boleyn

Not having the Pope as leader of the church was a big change from traditional Catholic beliefs. People who wanted religion to move away from Catholic beliefs were known as Protestants.

The 17-year-old Mary was furious about these changes because she liked the traditional Catholic way of doing things. What made it even worse was that Henry declared Mary **illegitimate**, to clear the way for children from his marriage to the woman he now loved, Anne, to become king or queen. Mary even lost the title of "Princess Mary" and was now known simply as "The Lady Mary".

Enter Elizabeth

Henry was overjoyed when Anne became pregnant and put plans in place for a huge celebration: he was convinced the baby would be a boy. There was only one problem – Anne gave birth to a daughter, Elizabeth, in September 1533.

the young Elizabeth

The celebrations were cancelled, but Henry still made it clear that Elizabeth was more important than his first daughter, Mary.

Anne became pregnant twice more, but both times the baby died before it was born. Henry became worried that, as with Katherine, he'd never be able to have a son with Anne. He wouldn't wait as long as he did with Katherine before moving on to his next wife.

Less than three years after they'd married, Anne was accused of having relationships with other men behind the king's back. In 1536, when Elizabeth was just two years old, Anne was executed. Like her half-sister Mary, Elizabeth was declared illegitimate and lost the title of Princess. Days after Anne's execution, Henry married his third wife, Jane Seymour.

the execution of Anne Boleyn

11

Arrival of a son

Henry married Jane Seymour in May 1536. In September 1537, Jane gave birth to a son, Edward. But Henry's joy didn't last long, as tragedy struck and Jane died two weeks later from an infection.

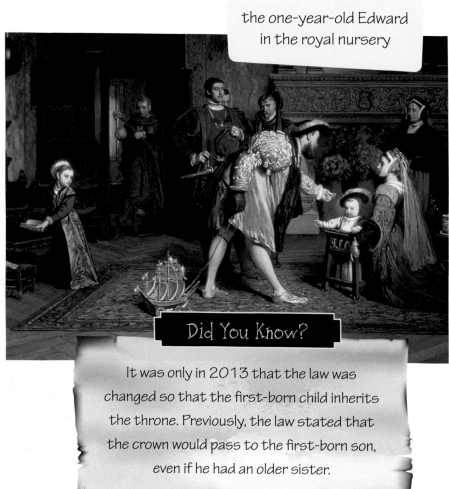

the one-year-old Edward in the royal nursery

Did You Know?

It was only in 2013 that the law was changed so that the first-born child inherits the throne. Previously, the law stated that the crown would pass to the first-born son, even if he had an older sister.

Although Henry married three more times, he didn't have any more children, so, in 1547, when he died, Edward became king, at the age of only nine.

the **coronation** of Edward the Sixth

Things were better for both of Henry's daughters by 1547 because he'd said that they were no longer illegitimate. The crown could pass to them, but only if Edward didn't have any children. Henry would have hoped that Edward would have a son to pass the crown to, but by 1553, the 15-year-old King Edward the Sixth was seriously ill.

Henry the Eighth's family, from left to right: Mary, Edward, Henry, Jane Seymour and Elizabeth, showing the importance of Henry's son above his daughters

While Edward was king, he made many changes to the religious traditions of England. This was because he was a Protestant, rather than a Catholic. Church services were now in English instead of Latin, priests no longer had to dress in fancy, brightly coloured clothes and they were even allowed to get married. And, just as his father had been, Edward was head of the Church, not the Pope.

Mary had never agreed with all these changes and Edward knew that if she became queen she'd want things to go back to how they were before. Edward was desperate to stop this happening so, as he got sicker, he came up with a plan to stop her becoming queen.

The nine-day queen

Edward decided to go against his father's will
by declaring Mary illegitimate again and making
a distant cousin, Lady Jane Grey, his chosen **successor**.
But, when Edward died of **tuberculosis** in July 1553,
Lady Jane only reigned for nine days.

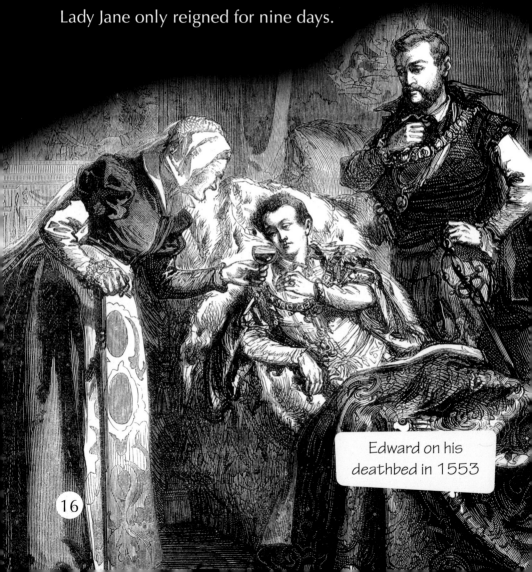

Edward on his
deathbed in 1553

Many important **nobles** decided that it was wrong to go against Henry's will, so they declared Mary the true queen. On 3 August 1553, Mary rode into London with a huge procession, including her half-sister Elizabeth, to be greeted by her loyal **subjects**. Lady Jane Grey, the nine-day queen, was put in prison in the Tower of London, and eventually executed.

Mary and Elizabeth enter London in 1553.

17

Mary's troublesome reign

Mary's road to power had been a difficult one and her time as queen would be no easier. She wanted to force everyone to go back to the traditional Catholic ways of doing things. However, many people were now against this, so she burned around 285 Protestants for disagreeing with her, gaining the nickname "Bloody Mary".

the persecution of Protestants during Mary's reign

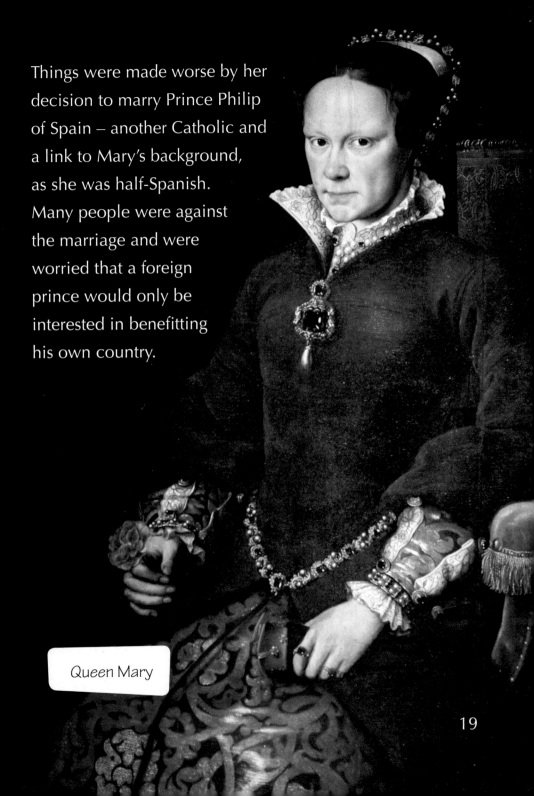

Things were made worse by her decision to marry Prince Philip of Spain – another Catholic and a link to Mary's background, as she was half-Spanish. Many people were against the marriage and were worried that a foreign prince would only be interested in benefitting his own country.

Queen Mary

Wyatt's rebellion

When he heard about Mary's proposed marriage to Philip, a nobleman called Thomas Wyatt launched a **rebellion** in 1554 to try to **overthrow** Mary and make Elizabeth queen instead.

Thomas Wyatt

Wyatt was a Protestant and wanted religion to stay as it had been under Edward. As Elizabeth was a Protestant, he hoped that this would happen if she were queen. Wyatt and his supporters marched to London, but Mary refused to flee and made an inspiring speech that kept the people loyal to her and led to the defeat of the rebels.

Wyatt was tortured to try to get him to admit that Elizabeth knew about his plans to overthrow Mary, but he always denied it. He even spoke about Elizabeth's innocence as part of the final words he was allowed to say to the crowd gathered to watch his execution for **high treason**.

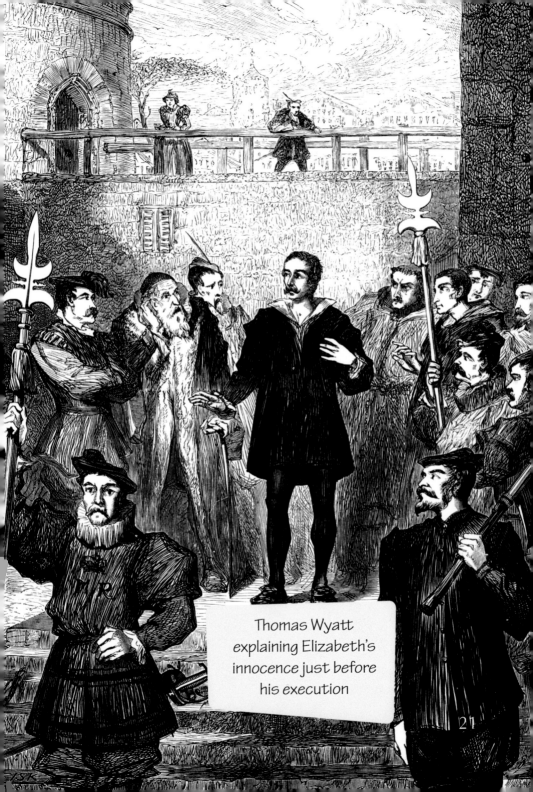

Thomas Wyatt explaining Elizabeth's innocence just before his execution

21

Elizabeth in danger

Wyatt's rebellion made Mary think that Elizabeth was involved in plans to try to gain power, so she had her imprisoned in the Tower of London.

Elizabeth wrote to Mary from prison to plead her innocence, and after two months she was released.

Elizabeth imprisoned in the Tower of London

23

A childless marriage

Mary married Philip on 25 July 1554, just two days after they'd met for the first time. Mary wanted to have a child to pass her throne on to so that the Catholic religious changes that she'd made would be kept. If she died childless, the throne would pass to the Protestant Elizabeth.

Philip of Spain

In September 1554, Mary's doctor announced that she was pregnant and that the baby was due in June 1555. The due date came and went, but Mary never gave birth. Even though she had many of the symptoms of pregnancy, it turned out she wasn't pregnant – this is known as a "phantom pregnancy". Mary would never allow what happened to be spoken about and it badly damaged her relationship with Philip. He spent more and more time back in Spain. After a second phantom pregnancy, Mary died childless in November 1558. She was 42 years old.

Mary and her husband Philip,
not long before she died

Mary's reign had been short and is mainly remembered
for the **ruthlessness** she showed in trying to force people
to follow her Catholic religion. It was now Elizabeth's turn
to rule England and she would do it for much longer,
and much more successfully, than her half-sister.

Queen Elizabeth

Elizabeth was 25 when she became queen in 1558. She would rule England for 45 years. Her coronation took place at Westminster Abbey and was a huge celebration. Elizabeth walked on a blue carpet from Westminster Palace to the Abbey and the crowd ripped up the carpet after she'd walked past, hoping for a souvenir of the day.

This portrait of Elizabeth was painted on her coronation.

Did You Know?

Elizabeth's coronation festival cost nearly £17,000, which would be over £3.5 million in today's money.

the coronation
of Elizabeth I

Dealing with religion

The religious service that took place at Elizabeth's coronation gave people a good idea of how she was going to deal with one of her key problems – deciding what type of religion the people of England should follow. The service took from both the Catholic and Protestant religions: it had parts in Latin and parts in English.

England did become a Protestant country again – because Elizabeth was put back in charge of the Church of England, which reversed the changes that Mary had made. However, Elizabeth didn't make as many Protestant changes to traditional beliefs as her half-brother, Edward, had done.

So, religion in her reign was seen as a "via media", meaning "middle way" in Latin. It was more of a compromise between Catholic and Protestant beliefs and, therefore, kept more of her subjects happy than Edward and Mary had managed with their extreme changes. Most importantly, Elizabeth said that she wouldn't "make windows into men's souls", meaning that as long as people followed her laws on religion in public, she didn't mind what they believed in private.

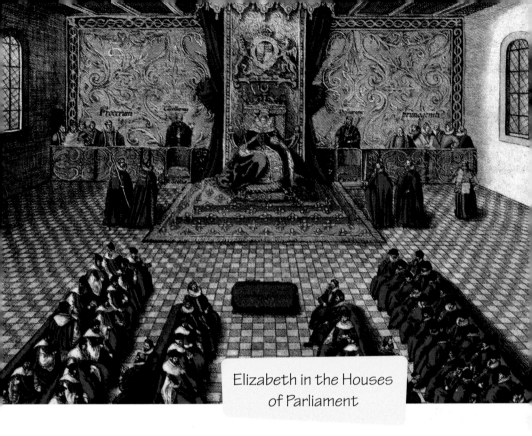

Elizabeth in the Houses
of Parliament

Elizabeth's compromise was very clever and was
a huge success; it made sure that there was no major
fighting between Catholics and Protestants in England
about religion during her reign.

However, though most of her subjects were happy with
the religious compromise, there were still some who
wanted to make England a Catholic country again.
Elizabeth had to deal with plots to overthrow her and
an attempted invasion of her country.

Plots

The most serious plots against Elizabeth involved her cousin, Mary, Queen of Scots. Mary had been queen of Scotland, which at this time was a separate country from England, with its own royal family. Nine years into Elizabeth's reign, in 1567, Mary was forced to flee Scotland after her husband was murdered and she married the man accused of his murder.

Mary fled to England, but as a Catholic and a relation of Elizabeth's with a distant claim to the throne, Elizabeth put her under house arrest for 19 years to remove the threat of her trying to take power. Eventually, in February 1587, Mary was executed, after letters were discovered from her to a group plotting to **assassinate** Elizabeth.

Did You Know?

One of Mary's dogs was said to have been hiding under her skirt as she was executed and then refused to leave her body until it was dragged away by force.

Mary Queen of Scots being led to her execution in 1587

The Spanish Armada

Elizabeth faced her greatest challenge in 1588:
an invasion by a fleet of 130 Spanish ships
known as an Armada.

the Spanish Armada,
which threatened England
in July 1588

The attack was ordered by Philip of Spain. His aim was to capture England and make it a Catholic country again. Following the execution of Mary, Queen of Scots, he wanted to stop Elizabeth killing any more Catholics. He claimed a right to the English throne because he'd been married to Elizabeth's half-sister, Mary, when she was queen.

Luckily for Elizabeth, the Armada was a complete failure. England sent burning barges towards the Spanish ships when they were in a port in France, just across the English Channel. To avoid being set on fire, the Armada fled quickly and didn't have time to prepare themselves against further attack.

The fleet became spread out and the smaller, more **manoeuvrable** English ships were able to strike. Bad weather forced the remaining ships to flee north up the east coast of England and the Spanish called off the invasion, with only half of them making it back to Spain.

No marriage, no heir

One of the things that Elizabeth is most famous for is her decision not to marry, which meant she never had an heir to pass her throne to. No one is completely sure of the reason for this.

Some believe that it was because she was traumatised by her father's execution of her mother, Anne Boleyn, and by his harsh treatment of his other wives. Others think that it was because it wasn't possible for Elizabeth to marry the one man she ever really loved, Robert Dudley. Dudley was at first married to someone else, but even when his wife died in 1560 after falling down some stairs, Elizabeth couldn't marry him, as he was suspected of his wife's murder.

Robert Dudley, the man many people believe Elizabeth truly loved

Perhaps the real reason for Elizabeth's decision not to marry was that she didn't want to be seen as **inferior** to a husband. Elizabeth made her views on marriage quite clear when she said that she'd prefer to be a "beggar woman and single than queen and married".

Even so, throughout her reign Elizabeth cleverly used the possibility of marriage to keep important people in Europe interested and friendly. This helped to keep England safe.

Did You Know?

Elizabeth kept the last letter Dudley ever wrote to her in 1588 for the rest of her life in her bedside treasure box.

Culture and exploration

Elizabeth's reign has been called a "Golden Age" because the stability she brought to England meant there was money available for journeys of discovery.

Explorers such as Sir Francis Drake and Sir Walter Raleigh did very well during this time. Raleigh led many expeditions to America and brought potatoes back to England for the first time – it is believed that he gave Elizabeth a potato plant as a present.

Sir Francis Drake

Drake was the first Englishman to sail around the entire world, in his ship called the *Golden Hinde*. The discoveries that these explorers made helped to make England a wealthy country.

Did You Know?

A model of the *Golden Hinde* is moored on the River Thames in London. Since it was built in 1973, it has sailed over 225,000 kilometres, which is the same as going around the world five times.

the model of
the *Golden Hinde*

There was huge success and **prosperity** at home in England too. Elizabeth loved the theatre and encouraged the playwright William Shakespeare to write many of his famous plays, which are still performed to this day. She enjoyed private performances of his work and donated a lot of money to his theatre group, which meant his plays could be widely performed and enjoyed by her subjects. The famous Globe Theatre was built in London in 1599, four years before Elizabeth died. The theatre is still popular today – more than 400 years later.

the original Globe Theatre in London

Did You Know?

The original Globe theatre burnt down in 1613 and an exact model was built in 1997.

Sister queens united

Mary and Elizabeth both had challenging journeys to becoming queen, but that is where the similarities end.

Unlike Mary's, Elizabeth's reign is seen as a huge success because she created religious stability in England. While Mary was seen as controlled by her husband, Elizabeth was viewed as an incredibly strong

queen who stood up to the most powerful country in the world at the time, Spain.

Her nickname, "Good Queen Bess", was certainly more flattering than her sister's, but her success might not have been possible without Mary leading the way as England's first queen.

After Elizabeth's death in 1603, her coffin was placed on top of her half-sister's in Westminster Abbey. These sisters, now united in death, had changed history as the first queens of England.

the final resting place of both Mary and Elizabeth

Glossary

assassinate	to murder someone, especially a politically well-known person
coronation	a ceremony that marks the formal crowning of a king or queen
high treason	committing a crime that threatens the safety of your country
illegitimate	a child born to unmarried parents
inferior	a person of lower rank or status
manoeuvrable	able to change position quickly and easily
nobles	people belonging by birth to the highest social class
overthrow	to take over from someone
Pope	the head of the Catholic Church
prosperity	the kind of success that comes from having a lot of money
rebellion	when people rise up and fight against those in power
ruthlessness	cruelty, showing no pity for others
subjects	people who live in a particular country under the rule of a king or queen
successor	someone who takes over a position or a job after another person
tuberculosis	a serious, sometimes fatal, infectious disease that mainly affects the lungs

Index

The Tudors 1509–1603

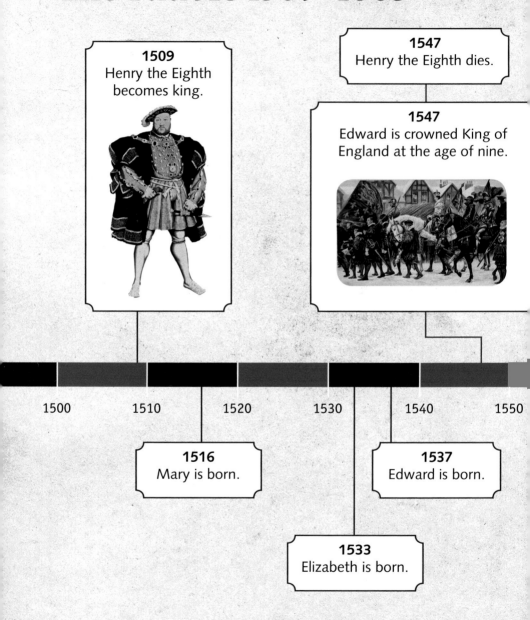

1509
Henry the Eighth becomes king.

1547
Henry the Eighth dies.

1547
Edward is crowned King of England at the age of nine.

1500   1510   1520   1530   1540   1550

1516
Mary is born.

1537
Edward is born.

1533
Elizabeth is born.

1558
Mary dies aged 42.

1558
Elizabeth is crowned
Queen of England.

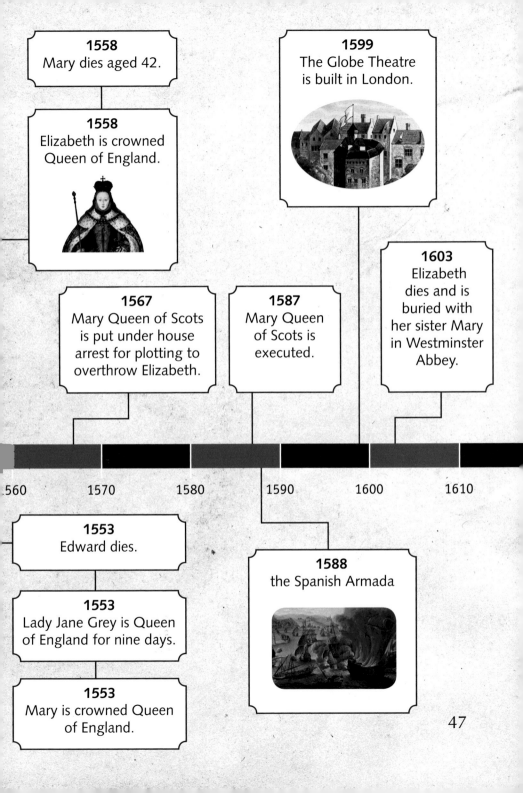

1599
The Globe Theatre
is built in London.

1567
Mary Queen of Scots
is put under house
arrest for plotting to
overthrow Elizabeth.

1587
Mary Queen
of Scots is
executed.

1603
Elizabeth
dies and is
buried with
her sister Mary
in Westminster
Abbey.

560   1570   1580   1590   1600   1610

1553
Edward dies.

1553
Lady Jane Grey is Queen
of England for nine days.

1553
Mary is crowned Queen
of England.

1588
the Spanish Armada

47

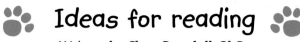

Ideas for reading

Written by Clare Dowdall, PhD
Lecturer and Primary Literacy Consultant

Reading objectives:
- read books that are structured in different ways
- discuss words and phrases that capture the reader's interest and imagination
- ask questions to improve understanding
- retrieve and record information from non-fiction

Spoken language objectives:
- participate in discussions, presentations, performances, role play, improvisations and debates

Curriculum links: History – Tudors; Art – portraits

Resources: painting materials; ICT for research and presentation

Build a context for reading

- Look at the front cover and read the title. Ask children to share what they know about the sister queens, Mary and Elizabeth.
- Check that children understand the phrase "lives and reigns". Explain what it means if necessary.
- Read the blurb together. Help children to identify each queen in the illustration and talk about the Tudor context. Ask children to think about why no-one imagined that a girl would take to the throne.

Understand and apply reading strategies

- Turn to the contents. Read through it as a group and ask children to describe how this information book is organised.
- Read p2 to the children. Ask children to raise a question that they will aim to answer as they read on.